LITTLE BOOK
OF NETER

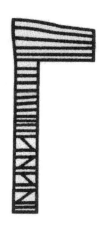

Little Book of Neter
CM BOOK PUBLISHING
www.Egyptianyoga.com
PO Box 570459, Miami, Fl 33257 Tel. (305) 378-6253

Little Book of Neter by Muata Ashby
ISBN 1-884564-58-5
© 2005 Sema Institute

Sema Institute of Yoga

Sema (⚮) is an Ancient Egyptian word and symbol meaning union. The Sema Institute is dedicated to the propagation of the universal teachings of spiritual evolution which relate to the union of humanity and the union of all things within the universe. It is an organization that recognizes the unifying principles in all spiritual and religious systems of evolution throughout the world. Our primary goals are to provide the wisdom of ancient spiritual teachings from the Neterian Culture of Ancient Africa in books, courses and other forms of communication. The Institute is open to all who believe in the principles of peace, non-violence and spiritual emancipation regardless of sex, race, or creed. The Sema Institute is recognized by the United States of America Internal Revenue Service as a Nonprofit Spiritual Organization with 501(C3) status. All donations to the Sema Institute are tax deductible.

ABOUT SEBAI MAA

Muata Ashby holds a Doctor of Philosophy Degree in World Religion and Myth, focusing on African and Indian Religion, and a Doctor of Divinity Degree in Holistic Healing. He is also a Pastoral Counselor and Teacher of Yoga Philosophy and Discipline. Dr. Ashby received his Doctor of Divinity Degree from and is an adjunct faculty member of the American Institute of Holistic Theology and the Florida International University. Dr. Ashby is a certification as a PREP Relationship Counselor. Dr. Ashby has been an independent researcher and practitioner of Egyptian, Indian and Chinese Yoga and psychology as well as Christian Mysticism. Dr. Ashby has engaged in Post Graduate research in Yoga at the Yoga Research Foundation. He has extensively studied mystical religious traditions from around the world and is an accomplished lecturer, artist, poet, screenwriter, playwright and author of over 40 books on yoga and spiritual philosophy. He and his partner Seba Dja Ashby are Ordained Ministers and Spiritual Counselors of Shetaut Neter and also the founder the Sema Institute, a non-profit organization dedicated to spreading the wisdom of Yoga and the Ancient Egyptian mystical traditions.

Dr. Muata Ashby has dedicated his life to educating all those interested in the mystical teachings of Yoga philosophy from Ancient Egypt. He conducts classes in Miami Florida on all aspects of Yoga wisdom and lifestyle.

TABLE OF CONTENTS

Sema Institute of Yoga

WHO ARE WE AND WHAT IS OR MISSION?

Lets begin here, with "Who are we?" What is the Sema Institute all about? What is Neterianism? Is it a philosophy, a school, a cult, or a religious program? What is it?

If you are going to the class to study Neterian philosophy, you go out into the street and someone asks you, "What are you up to? You go to this place for a couple of hours. What are you doing over there? Something mysterious? Something wild? Or something crazy? What is it that you are doing? What are you going to tell them; I am in a cult? Or I am doing some secret philosophy.

Neterianism is not a church. Neterianism is not a cult. Neterianism is not New Age spirituality...trying to put all the spirits together and trying to say "Oh, we are all one". New Age spirituality is really a reaction to the oppression of Orthodox Religion, an attempt to move away from religion all together. Thus, it is not an authentic spiritual movement, but in a sense, more like a new form of limited religious practice.

True religion (authentic spiritual movement) is a process that leads you through three steps: myth, ritual and mysticism. If one's religion does not have these three steps, then one is not practicing true religion. If a religion has a myth and its followers practice ritual(s) relating to that myth, if that is the extent of the religion, only containing dogmas and stories in which its followers must have faith, then that religion is not reaching a mystical level of oneness with all creation. Such a religion stays at the level of ritual, and leads to conflict with other religions that have different rituals...each fighting with the other over which is the holiest and or true ritual, and which is the only true myth. This is a source of strife between religions.

Practicing Neterianism means that one is practicing Kamitan African Religion. That is how you can define it. There are two branches to our organization. One is the Sema Institute. Under this branch we have Sema University, where we now have an Associate Degree program for advanced education, the bookstore, audio tapes, video tapes...everything that relates to the academic-educational aspect of the Sema Institute.

Secondly, we have the Temple of Shetaut Neter/ Temple of Aset. This includes everything related to priesthood, spiritual counseling, initiations, and spiritual worship programs. I want you to understand it this way, so that you can realize that the teaching can be approached as a philosophy of life, a spiritual philosophy or as a religion, a spiritual religious process. So when someone asks you, what you are practicing, how will you answer? What would a person practicing Yoruba religion say if asked this question? What would a person practicing Voodum say if asked this question? They would respond, "I am practicing African Religion" or "I am practicing Yoruba." Thus, if you choose to join the practice, you can say I am practicing Neterianism.

It is very important for you to realize this term "Shetaut Neter" comes directly from the scriptures of Ancient Africa...from the Medu Neter itself. It is not a made up term. It is not a fabricated term for modern times. It is the actual term. In ancient times, Shetaut Neter was practiced in the land that is currently in modern times called "Egypt," but the African name is "Kamit."

However, it must be clearly understood that in Neterian Theology there are two kinds of Mysteries, the lower and the higher. The lower Mysteries are worldly, practical branches of learning, the areas that help human beings to improve their lives and learn about the world around them. The lower mysteries offer limited insight because they only use physical, empirical means for the researches. Examples of the lower mysteries include mechanics, engineering, astronomy, literature, mathematics, physiology, etc. The higher Mysteries are the disciplines or sciences that promote insight into the nature of self and the revelation of the Mysteries of life, the Mysteries of the universe. The higher Mysteries answer questions such as "Who am I? Where did I come from? Why am I here? What is life? What or who is God?," etc. This book does not deal with the lower mysteries. However, certain knowledge of the lower Mysteries is necessary to pursue the higher Mysteries. One could not study the Mysteries if one could not understand a certain level of mathematics, language, etc.; a certain level of maturity, stability and intellectual capacity are necessary to pursue higher spiritual attainment, and the lower Mysteries provide that foundation. By being proficient in one of the lower Mysteries, you can get a reasonably well paying job, and pay your bills. Then you can also to afford to buy spiritual books, to read them and then reflect on their meaning. Stability and financial capacity gained from being proficient in the lower Mysteries allows you to think without the pressure of financial burdens, purchase the materials necessary for the practice, visit spiritual centers, confer with spiritual teachers, etc. So this book is for those who want to know more and be introduced to the higher Mysteries of life, the mystical, metaphysical disciplines that lead to attaining transcendental consciousness, enlightenment, the Great Spiritual Awakening.

Shetaut Neter: The Path of Awakening

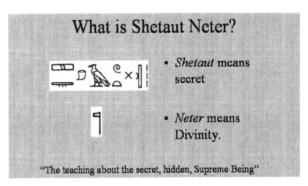

What is Shetaut Neter?

- *Shetaut* means secret

- *Neter* means Divinity.

"The teaching about the secret, hidden, Supreme Being"

Long ago, before any other civilization on earth arose, the Ancient Kamitian (Egyptian) Sages developed an extensive system of mythology and psychology as a means to assist human beings to develop to their full potential. This philosophy was called *Smai Taui* or *Smai Heru Set* (Egyptian Yoga). Who am I and what is this universe? These are questions which have perplexed humanity since the beginning of civilization. However, the Sages of ancient Africa were able to discover the secrets of the universe and of the innermost nature of the human heart. This discovery allowed them to create a civilization which lasted for tens of thousands of years and it enabled the creation of the magnificent monuments (Sphinx, Great Pyramids and Temples, which stand to this day. Also, Ancient Egyptian religion influenced and continues to influence the religions of Africa and other world religions of today such as Christianity, Hinduism and Islam. So what does this mean for us today? Many people have visited Egypt and have studied the work of Egyptologists but how many have been transformed into higher minded, more content, more powerful human beings who can rise to the challenges of life and aspire to achieve material and spiritual success? Many people have read about and studied Ancient Egyptian mythology but how is it possible to gain a deeper understanding of the mystical principles and how is it possible to integrate them into one's life so as to transform oneself into a higher being as the texts describe? How is it possible to go beyond the limited understanding of religion and the philosophy of modern culture which have not brought peace and prosperity to the world? In order to Succeed in Shetaut Neter one must also practice the Sema Tawi (Yoga) disciplines. When one practices the disciplines of Sema Tawi in Shetaut Neter this is called *Shedy* or *"Studies and practices to penetrate the mysteries."*

Who is Neter?

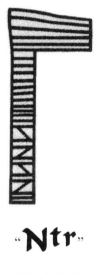

"Ntr"

Who is Ntr?

The symbol of Neter was described by an Ancient Kamitan sage as:

"That which is placed in the coffin"

The term Ntr , or Ntjr , come from the Ancient Egyptian hieroglyphic language which did not record its vowels. However, the term survives in the Coptic language as *"Nutar."* The same Coptic meaning (divine force or sustaining power) applies in the present as it did in ancient times, It is a symbol composed of a wooden staff that was wrapped with strips of fabric, like a mummy. The strips alternate in color with yellow, green and blue. The mummy in Kamitan

7

spirituality is understood to be the dead but resurrected Divinity. So the Nutar is actually every human being who does not really die, but goes to live on in a different form. Further, the resurrected spirit of every human being is that same Divinity. Phonetically, the term Nutar is related to other terms having the same meaning, the latin "Natura," Spanish Naturalesa, English "Nature" and "Nutriment", etc. In a real sense, as we will see, Natur means power manifesting as Neteru and the Neteru are the objects of creation, i.e. "nature."

What is Shetaut Neter? The Ancient Egyptians were African peoples who lived in the north-eastern quadrant of the continent of Africa. They were descendants of the Nubians, who had themselves originated from farther south into the heart of Africa at the great lakes region, the sources of the Nile River. They created a vast civilization and culture earlier than any other society in known history and organized a nation which was based on the concepts of balance and order as well as spiritual enlightenment. These ancient African people called their land Kamit and soon after developing a well ordered society they began to realize that the world is full of wonders but life is fleeting and that there must be something more to human existence. They developed spiritual systems that were designed to allow human beings to understand the nature of this secret being who is the essence of all Creation. They called this spiritual system "Shtaut Ntr."

The term "Neterianism"

is derived from the name "Shetaut Neter." What is Neterianism? The term "Neterianism" is derived from the term Shetaut Neter. Those who follow the spiritual path of Shetaut Neter are referred to as "Neterians." When referring to the religion of ancient Egypt, itself, the term Neterianism will be used. This term will be substituted for or will be used interchangeably with the term Ancient Egyptian Religion or Kamitan Religion or spirituality. All these are referring to the same thing: Neterianism, Shetaut Neter, Ancient Egyptian Religion, or Kamitan Religion.

Those who follow the spiritual path of Shetaut Neter are therefore referred to as "Neterians."

Neterianism is the science of Neter, that is, the study of the secret or mystery of Neter, the enigma of that which transcends ordinary consciousness but from which all creation arises. The world did not come from nothing, nor is it sustained by nothing. Rather it is a manifestation of that which is beyond time and space but which at the same time permeates and maintains the fundamental elements. In other words, it is the substratum of Creation and the essential nature of all that exists.

Etymology of the term Shetaut Neter

Here we have the term *Shetaut* or *Sheta* meaning "hidden, difficult to understand, hard to get through, a mystery." The term *Shetaut Kepheru*, means hidden, creator of forms; *Shetitu* means: "writings related to the hidden teachings"; *Shet-Ta* means "the land covered by the Nile." When the Nile water is overflowing, the land is covered, so it means covered, or shrouded.

Sheta means "the secret hidden Divinity." *Shetaut Aset* means "the Divinity in the hidden abode or throne;" (Aset means abode or throne). *Shetai* means "hidden secret Being, The Divine essential nature." This is the etymology of the term Shetaut in Shetaut Neter.

The Goal of Shetaut Neter: The Great Awakening

What is the purpose of Neterianism? What is the purpose of all the disciplines of Neterian spirituality?

The end of all the Neterian disciplines is to discover the meaning of "Who am I," to unravel the mysteries of life and to fathom the depths of eternity and infinity. This is the task of all human beings and it is to be accomplished in this very lifetime.

This can be done by learning the ways of the Neteru, emulating them and finally becoming like them, Akhus, (enlightened beings), walking the earth as giants and accomplishing great deeds such as the creation of the universe!

The Kemetic word "Nehast" means attaining that sublime and highest goal of life which is Spiritual Enlightenment, to experience the state of conscious awareness of oneness with the Divine and all Creation which transcends individuality born of ego consciousness...like the river uniting with the ocean, discovering the greater essential nature of Self... that state which bestows abiding blessedness, peace, bliss, contentment, fulfillment, freedom from all limitation and supreme empowerment.

The ultimate goal of life is *Nehast*. Nehast means "Spiritual Awakening." It is the spiritual awakening that leads one to discover the glory of life beyond death, discovering immortality, eternity and supreme peace. This is the coveted goal of all spiritual aspirants in all religions of the world, past or present. This is the goal that is to be striven for in life. It is the most worthy goal because all else will fade away one day. All else is perishable, fleeting and illusory. And this is what is called the Great Awakening, Nehast, the Awakening to spiritual consciousness. In the upper left hand corner of the slide you can see Asar Awakening from the tomb being assisted by the four sons of Heru. These four sons are also the first Shemsu, the Shemsu Heru. They are the ones who follow Asar, and they help to resurrect him. Nehast means to wake-up, to awaken to the higher existence.

The question is how to attain that lofty goal (Nehast). Just because all religions are striving for that does not mean they are engaging the correct methods to achieve that goal. They may have the dogma, the idea, but that does not mean that they have the how. One cannot attain resurrection, the spiritual awakening, just by faith. Faith must be followed by action, living in accordance with the teachings. That leads to growing understanding of and finally experience of the Divine. The end of all of the Neterian disciplines is to discover the meaning of "Who am I?," to unravel the mysteries of life, and to fathom the depths of eternity and infinity. This is the task of all human beings, and it is to be accomplished in this very lifetime. This can be done by learning the ways of the Neteru and emulating them, and finally becoming like them, Akhus walking the earth as giants and accomplishing great deeds.

Akhu is a term that we use in Neterian Theology that means "enlightened beings." Akhu is a person who has achieved Nehast, who has achieved awakening...the great Enlightenment.

The Follower of Neterianism

"Shemsu Neter"

"Follower (of) Neter"

The term "Neterianism" is derived from the name "Shetaut Neter." Those who follow the spiritual path of Shetaut Neter are therefore referred to as "Neterians."

Neterianism is the science of Neter, that is, the study of the secret or mystery of Neter, the enigma of that which transcends ordinary consciousness but from which all creation arises. The world did not come from nothing, nor is it sustained by nothing. Rather it is a manifestation of that which is beyond time and space but which at the same time permeates and maintains the fundamental elements. In other words, it is the substratum of Creation and the essential nature of all that exists.

So those who follow the Neter may be referred to as Neterians.

Where Was Shetaut Neter Practiced in Ancient Times?

In ancient times Neterianism, was practice in the land of Kamit and the land of Kush. Kamit is located in the Northeastern corner of Africa. A civilization began to appear along the Nile River more than 12,000 years ago; this civilization became the Kamitan society. The Kamitans themselves say that they came from the south, from the land of Kush, originally as colonists.

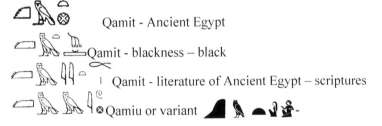

Qamit - Ancient Egypt

Qamit - blackness – black

Qamit - literature of Ancient Egypt – scriptures

Qamiu or variant

Ancient Egyptians-people of the black land.

Who Was the Founder of Neterianism?

One of the most important questions in life for followers of any religion is who started it? In order to understand who founded Neterianism, the teaching of Shetaut Neter, we must also understand the origins of creation. In the sacred scriptures of Shetaut Neter we are told that Creation is a cycle. That is, that Creation occurs cyclically. God brings creation into existence and then dissolves it again.

LORD KHEPRI, FOUNDER OF NETERIANISM

The current cycle of Creation began around the year 36,000 B.C.E. In the beginning there was nothing more than a watery mass, a primeval ocean, called Nun. Nun is the body of Khepri. Prior to the creation, Khepri remained in a recumbent posture. He rested on the back of the great serpent *Asha-hrau* ("many faces").

In the form of Ra Khepri arose from the primeval ocean (Nun) with his boat, accompanied by his company of Gods and Goddesses. Nun lifted the boat from the depths of the ocean so it could engender Creation and sail for millions of years..

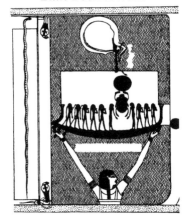

From that Nun the Divine Spirit arose by stimulating Asha-hrau to move and churn the ocean. Then he named himself Khepri, Creator. Khepri called out his own name and ⊗ ▭ *dchn* –vibrations were infused in the ocean and waves vere formed. Just as there are many waves in the ocean with many shapes and sizes, the objects of the world came into being in the form of elements, Ra (fire), Shu (air-space), Tefnut (water), Geb (earth), Nut (ether). Everything in creation emanates from the Nun or primordial ocean, and expresses in the form of elements in succeeding levels of denseness. These elements also manifest in the form of the opposites of Creation (man-woman, up-down, white-black) which appear to be exclusive and separate from each other, but which are in reality complements to each other.

Khepri and the Creation Myth

Khepri congealed the Nun, his own body, into all the forms of Creation. The first spot that was congealed from the Nun is called ▭▭▭ *Benben*, the first place, the Ben-Ben dot, •, of Creation. That dot is the center point in the symbol of Khepr-Ra ☉. That dot is the very point at the top of the Pyramid ▭ *mr*- Obelisk, 〜〜〜 *tekhnu*. The pyramid-obelisk symbolizes the mound that formed from that initial spot. Khepri sat atop the hill of Creation and all solid ground took form underneath him.

Khepri then bought forth Creation by emerging in a boat. The Nun waters lifted him and his boat up with his great arms. He brought nine divinities with him in that boat, lesser gods and goddesses, to help him sustain the Creation and lead human beings on the righteous path to life and spiritual enlightenment.

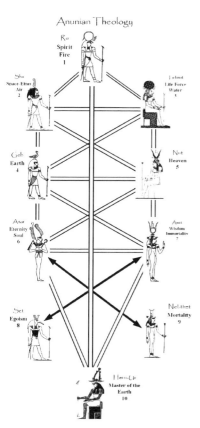

Anunian Theology

Ra
Spirit
Fire
1

Shu
Space-Ether
Air
2

Tefnut
Life Force
Water
3

Geb
Earth
4

Nut
Heaven
5

Asar
Eternity
Soul
6

Aset
Wisdom
Immortality
7

Set
Egoism
8

Nebthet
Mortality
9

Heru-Ur
Master of the
Earth
10

Having created Creation, Khepri now sails the ocean, which has now become Creation itself, with his divinities, on the divine boat. Khepri-Ra and the *pauti*, Company of gods and goddesses, travels in the Boat of Millions of Years, which traverses the heavens, and thereby sustains creation through the wake of the boat that sends ripples (vibrations) throughout Creation. The act of "Sailing" signifies the motion in creation. Motion implies that events occur in the realm of time and space relative to each other, thus, the phenomenal universe comes into existence as a mass of moving essence we call the elements. Prior to this motion, there was the primeval state of being without any form and without existence in time or space. The gods and goddesses of the boat form the court of

15

Kheper-Ra. As Ra, the Supreme Being governed the earth for many thousands of years. He created the world, the planets, the stars and the galaxies; he also created animals, as well as men and women. In the beginning, men and women revered the Divine, but after living for a very long time, they began to take Ra for granted. They became arrogant and vain. Ra sent his daughter, Hetheru, to punish them, but she forgot her way and became lost in the world. Then He left for his abode in heaven and gave the earthly throne to his son Shu, and daughter, Tefnut. After a long period of time, they turned over the throne to their children, Geb and Nut. After some time again, Geb and Nut gave the throne to their children, Asar and Aset, and so on in a line of succession throughout history, down to the Pharaohs of Kamit.

Lord Khepri manifests as Neberdjer, "All-encompassing Divinity." Aspirants are to say:

tu-a m shems n Neberdjer
"I am a follower of Neberdjer

er sesh n Kheperu
in accordance with the writings of Lord Kheperu"

So, the Shetaut Neter "Mystery teachings" were originally given by the Creator, Khepri. In this capacity he is known as

 Shetaut Kheperu, "hidden Creator of forms." Lord Djehuti codified these Mystery teachings into the hieroglyphic texts, and these teachings were passed down to succeeding generations of divinities, sages and priests and priestesses throughout history.

So Lord Khepri imparted his knowledge to the divinities, and especially to his son Djehuti . Thus, Lord Khepri, the Self Created Divinity, is the founder of Shetaut Neter. The codifier was his first main disciple, Djehuti.

Djehuti has the body of a man and the head of an Ibis bird. He also has another form as a baboon. The teaching that Lord Khepri gave to Djehuti became known as *Shetitu* ⌐⌐ ı ı ıand it was conveyed through the *Medtu Neteru* (hieroglyphic texts).

"Meðtu Neteru"

The teachings of the Neterian Traditions are conveyed in the scriptures of the Neterian Traditions. The Medu Neter was used through all periods by priests and priestesses – mostly in monumental inscriptions such as the Pyramid texts, Obelisks, temple inscriptions, etc. – since Pre-Dynastic times. It is the earliest form of writing in known history. Thus, these Shetaut (mysteries- rituals, wisdom, philosophy) about the Neter (Supreme Being) are related in the writings of the hidden teaching. And those writings are referred to as *Medu Neter* or "Divine Speech," the writings of the god Djehuti (Ancient Egyptian god of the divine word). *Medu Neter* also generally refers to any Kamitan hieroglyphic texts or inscriptions. The term Medu Neter makes use of a special hieroglyph, , which means "*medu*" or "staff - walking stick-speech." This means that speech is the support for the Divine, . Thus, just as the staff supports an elderly person, the hieroglyphic writing (the word) is a prop or support (staff) which sustains the Divine in the realm of time and space. That is, these Divine writings (*Medu Neter*) contain the wisdom which enlightens us about the Divine, Shetaut Neter. If *Shetitu* is mastered through the study of the Medu Neter then the spiritual aspirant becomes Maakheru or true of thought, word and deed, that is, purified in body, mind and soul. The symbol medu is static while the symbol of Kheru is dynamic.

The term Maakheru uses the glyph kheru, which is a rudder – oar (rowing), and a symbol of voice, meaning that purification occurs through the righteous movement of the word, when it is used (rowing-movement) to promote Maat (virtue, order, peace, harmony and truth). So Medu Neter is the potential word and Maa kheru is the perfected word.

The hieroglyphic texts (Medu Neter) become useful (Maakheru) in the process of religion when they are used as *hekau* - the Ancient Egyptian "Words of Power." They are to be *Hesi*, chanted and *Shmai-* sung, and thereby one performs *Dua* or adoration of the Divine. The divine word allows the speaker to control the gods and goddesses, who actually are the cosmic forces in Creation. Human beings are a higher order beings, and they can attain this higher state of consciousness if they learn about the nature of the universe and elevate themselves through virtue and wisdom.

Above: Lord Djehuti imparted the teaching he learned from Khepri to goddess Hetheru (here in the form of a cow goddess). She became lost in the world and forgot her true identity. He showed her how to discover her true Self, how to know herself and how to find her way back to heaven, to her father Ra. Here Djehuti is shown presenting to Hetheru, the healed right eye of Ra, her true essence.

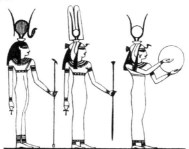

Above: Goddess Hetheru as Queen

Lord Khep-Ra knew that human beings needed guidance, so he sent his great grandchildren, Asar and Aset, to be teachers and role models for human beings on earth. Lord Djehuti also imparted the hidden knowledge of life to Aset and Asar, so that they would lead people on earth in a righteous manner, showing them the path of peace, prosperity and spiritual enlightenment. Asar and Aset established the Shetaut Neter, "Divine

Mysteries," ritual worship and Ancient Egyptian religion. When human beings become too involved in the world they forget their true nature, and so

the Temple, ![hieroglyphs] *Het Neter* {House of the Divinity {God(dess)}-Temple},was created, where the pressure of the world can be relieved, and an association with something other than the worldly perspective (i.e., with Divinity) can occur.

Such a place and its teaching are needed so that the mind can become aware of higher possibilities and turn away from ![hieroglyphs] *umt-ab-* "mental dullness" due to ![hieroglyphs] *Khemn*, "ignorance," and be led to ![hieroglyphs] *Nehast –*"Resurrection, spiritual awakening," ![hieroglyphs] *Akhu*, "enlightenment" and so that human beings may become ![hieroglyphs] *Sheps-* "nobility, honor, venerable-ness, honored ancestors."

Above: *Aset nurses baby Heru*

So, Aset learned the Mystery teachings from Lord Djehuti. Aset is the ancient African prototype of the mother and child which is popular all over Africa, and also in Christian and Indian iconography with the birth of Jesus and Krishna, respectively. The mother is the first teacher. Aset not only

raised Heru, but also initiated him into the mysteries of life and creation, with the teaching she learned from Djehuti and Khepri, in order to enlighten him and make him strong for the battle of life.

Heru is the redeemer, the challenger, the one who stands up for his father, Asar, and liberates him from the imprisonment of death. Heru represents spiritual aspiration and success in the spiritual path. Heru reestablishes order after defeating the evil Set, and takes the throne of Kamit. In his form as Heru Behdet, Heru is a warrior. He fights for truth, justice and freedom for all. Heru, the redeemer, the warrior, the greatest advocate of Asar (the soul) and triumphant aspirant is the one who leads the aspirant to the initiation hall. As seen above, Heru is often the one shown leading the aspirant by the hand, into the inner shrine. In rituals, the priest wears a Heru mask in the context of a ritual theatrical ceremony of the temple that is meant to awaken the glory of the Neterian teaching in the heart of the aspirant.

What is the purpose of life? In order to tread a true and beneficial path in life it is necessary to understand what is good in life and is worth pursuing, as opposed to what is not true or worth pursuing. The philosophy provides insight. The wisdom teachings related to this important issue need to be carefully studied and diligently reflected upon until the message is understood clearly by your mind.

Kamitan Proverbs:

"The purpose of human life is to achieve a state of consciousness apart from bodily concerns"

"Men and women are to become godlike through a life of virtue and cultivation of the spirit through scientific knowledge, practice, and bodily discipline."

"Salvation is freeing of the soul from the bodily fetters. Becoming a god through knowledge and wisdom, controlling the forces of the cosmos instead of being a slave to them. Subduing the lower nature and through awakening the higher Self, ending the cycle of rebirth and dwelling with the neters who direct and control the great plan."

What should be the purpose of life? Should the purpose of life be to get rich, to have lots of fame, or a big family? No, the purpose is to become God-like, and further, to become one with God!

Now, if you decide to adopt Shetaut Neter, and you meet, say, a Christian person on the road, how will you respond to them? Perhaps you have friends in your family who are Christians, Muslims, etc., and they may ask you what are you doing? You may answer: "I am practicing African Religion." "I am practicing Neterianism." Suppose they now ask you, "What is your goal in Neterianism?" Do not tell them you are trying to become a god or a goddess. Don't waste you time getting into that kind of conflict, because in their view only Jesus can do that. But in African Religion... everybody can do that, and not in some future time, but right now...in your lifetime.

In ancient times, there was a certain genre of literature called "The Harper's Songs." This is a special genre of ancient Egyptian literature that deals with the understanding of the meaning and purpose of life. Through the following Harper's Song, the purpose of life becomes clear. The song goes:

"I have heard these songs, which are in the ancient tombs
Which tell of the virtues of life on earth, and make little of life in the
        Neterkert (cemetery).
Why then do likewise to eternity?
It is a place of justice, without fear,
where an uproar is forbidden,
where no one attacks his fellow.
This place has no enemies;

21

All our relatives have lived in it from time immemorial.
and with millions more to come.
I joined in?

It is not possible to linger in Egypt
No one can escape from going west (note: west is the land to death, the
     land of the afterlife, the Netherworld)
One's acts on earth are like a dream
Welcome safe and sound,
   to whoever arises in the West"

The Harper is telling us we cannot linger on earth. We must plan for our
departure, and that our acts on earth here are like a dream. If you
consider what the Harper's Song is saying, it is like when you have
a dream when you are asleep. Your dream appears to be very real,
but when you wake up from it in the morning, then you realize that
it is not real. What happens when you go to sleep? When you go to
sleep you believe that dream world is real, and this waking world is
unreal. Which is the reality then? Do you see the high philosophy
that is going on here? It means that there is something within you
that is beyond the changing realms of consciousness... the waking
and the dream state.

How are you to discover that state that is beyond illusion? How are you to
elevate yourself to transcend this mortal finite existence?
Accomplishing this is what is referred to as becoming gods and
goddesses. The question then becomes how is this to be achieved?
It is wonderful for me to tell you what Shetaut Neter is all about.
But it is also important that you know how this is achieved. I am
sure that you have heard of that saying "many are called and few are
chosen."

Those of you who are studying this now, as opposed to the millions of
people who are out there in the world – you are reading this because
you are ready to pursue some new path to life. You are ready to
discover some insight that leads you to the answers to your
questions, and most likely, as to the true purpose in life and the
source of pain in life. I am mainly just confirming what you already
know anyway, because you have the wisdom inside you, but you
have to know how to tap into it.

What is Sema Tawi
"Sema Tawi or Smai Tawi"
(From Chapter 4 of the *Prt m Hru*)

In Chapter 4 and Chapter 17 of the *Prt m Hru*, a term "*Sma (Sema* or *Smai)* Tawi" is used. It means "Union of the two lands of Egypt," ergo "Egyptian Yoga." The two lands refer to the two main districts of the country (North and South). In ancient times, Egypt was divided into two sections or land areas. These were known as Lower and Upper Egypt. In Ancient Egyptian mystical philosophy, the land of Upper Egypt relates to the divinity Heru (Horus), who represents the Higher Self, and the land of Lower Egypt relates to Set, the divinity of the lower self. So *Sema (Smai) Tawi* means "the union of the two lands" or the "Union of the lower self with the Higher Self. The lower self relates to that which is negative and uncontrolled in the human mind including worldliness, egoism, ignorance, etc. (Set), while the Higher Self relates to that which is above temptations and is good in the human heart as well as in touch with Transcendental consciousness (Heru). Thus, we also have the Ancient Egyptian term *Sema (Smai) Heru-Set,* or the union of Heru and Set. So Sema (Smai) Tawi or Sema (Smai) Heru-Set are the Ancient Egyptian words which are to be translated as "Egyptian Yoga."

 **"Shedy"**

WHAT IS SHEDY?

Shedy means: "to penetrate the mysteries", "to study the teachings deeply and gain insight into their meaning." What Are The Disciplines of Shedy:

There were 4 aspects of Shedy (Spiritual Practice):
Sedjm -"Listening"
Maat -"Right Actions"

Uash - "Devotion to God"
Uaa -"Meditation"

For those who have chosen Shetaut Neter as their path, it is necessary to enter into a process called Shedy. Shedy means. Each discipline of Shedy is designed to inform, purify, elevate and establish the Shemsu on the path to awakening. These are the steps to the effective practice of religion that will lead a human being to maturity and spiritual realization. In order to be effective the disciplines must be listened to, acted upon and meditated upon under the correct guidance.

1-Listen to the teaching: **"Mestchert"** ⌐⏝⫶⧠ "Listening, to fill the ears, listen attentively"

2- Study, reflection on the teaching: **MAZIT** ⫶⧠⧠ "to think, to ponder, to fix attention, concentration" and right actions based on the teachings: Learn the path of Virtue, that is **Maat** ⧠⧠⧠. Even in your present circumstance learn to develop divine values, be righteous, treat others righteously and fairly, uphold truth and justice for all. This will purify you and will allow you to experience the benefits of steps 1-3 above. This is your duty. Uphold your responsibilities. Be a virtuous and you will discover inner peace and higher consciousness and you will also affect those around you. So it is very important to practice the teachings to the highest possible degree. Acquire the books that relate the teaching. If possible get audio taped lectures from qualified preceptors, that explain the teaching. Then your efforts will be most effective in transforming your life and discovering true redemption and divine glory.

3-Then Meditate upon the teaching: **Uaa** ⧠⧠⧠ "Meditation"

Little Book of Neter
The Neterian Creed: What I Believe
(based on the Scriptures and Traditions of Shetaut Neter)
By
Sebai Maa and Seba Dja Ashby

As a *Neterian,* I follow the Ancient African-Kamitan religious path of *Shetaut Neter,* which teaches about the mysteries of the Supreme Being, *Neberdjer,* the All Encompassing Divinity. I believe that from *Neberdjer* proceed all the *Neteru* (gods and goddesses), and all the worlds, and the entire universe. Since *Neberdjer* manifests as the *Neteru, Neberdjer* can be worshipped as a god or a goddess. I believe that there is only one Supreme Being, *Neberdjer,* and that the gods and goddesses are expressions of the One Supreme Being, *Neberdjer.* As a Neterian, I strive to come into harmony with the gods and goddesses, the *Neteru,* by developing within my personality the different virtuous and divine qualities they symbolize; this will lead me closer to *Neberdjer.* As a Neterian, I also believe that Supreme Being I call *Neberdjer* is the same Supreme Being that is worshiped by other religions under different names.

I believe that *Neberdjer* established all creation on *Maat,* righteousness, truth, and order, and that my actions, termed *Ari,* determine the quality of life I lead and experience. If I act with *Maat* (positive *Ari*) my path will be free of suffering and pain. When I forget *Maat* and act in an unrighteous manner (negative *Ari*), I invite suffering and pain into my life.

As a *Neterian* I believe when my body dies, my heart's actions will be examined against *Maat.* If it is found that I upheld *Maat* during my lifetime, I will have positive *Ari,* and my *Akhu* (spirit) will become one with *Neberdjer* for all eternity. This is called *Nehast,* the Spiritual Awakening-Enlightenment. If it is found that I acted with selfishness and greed, I will have negative *Ari,* and my *Ba* (soul) will suffer after death and then be reincarnated again to live in the world of time and space again. This is called *Uhemankh* (reincarnation).

As a *Neterian* I believe in the teaching of *Shemsu,* following the path of *Shetaut Neter,* by practicing the disciplines of *Shedy,* which include: Study of Wisdom teachings (*Rech-Ab*), Devotion to God (*Uashu*), Acting with Righteousness (*Maat*) and Meditation (*Uaa*). *Neberdjer* provided the *Shetitu,* the spiritual teaching that was written in *Medu Neter* (hieroglyphic scripture) so that the *Shemsu* (followers) might study the wisdom teaching of Shetaut Neter. Two most important *Neterian* scriptures are the *Pert M Hru* and the *Hessu Amun,* and the most important *Neterian* myth is the *Asarian* Resurrection.

By the practice of the disciplines of Shedy, I will discover the *Shetaut* (Mysteries) of life and become *Maakheru,* Pure of Heart. I will become one with God even before death, and I will discover supreme peace, abiding happiness and fulfillment of my life's purpose, and promote peace and harmony for the world.

**The Sema Institute and Temple of Shetaut Neter is dedicated to
The dissemination of Neterian Wisdom (Sema and Shetaut Neter) in books,
Neterianism is the modern day reference to Shetaut Neter (Ancient Egyptian Religion),
Promoting the practice of Shetaut Neter Religion
Training Neterian Aspirants,
Promoting World Peace, human dignity and equality between cultures, genders and the care of the environment.**

THE GENERAL PRINCIPLES OF SHETAUT NETER RELIGION
(Teachings Presented in the Kamitan scriptures)
What We Uphold

1. The Purpose of Life is to Attain the Great Awakening-Enlightenment-Know thyself.
2. SHETAUT NETER enjoins the Shedy (spiritual investigation) as the highest endeavor of life.
3. SHETAUT NETER enjoins that it is the responsibility of every human being to promote order and truth.
4. SHETAUT NETER enjoins the performance of Selfless Service to family, community and humanity.
5. SHETAUT NETER enjoins the Protection of nature.
6. SHETAUT NETER enjoins the Protection of the weak and oppressed.
7. SHETAUT NETER enjoins the Caring for hungry.
8. SHETAUT NETER enjoins the Caring for the homeless.
9. SHETAUT NETER enjoins the equality for all people.
10. SHETAUT NETER enjoins the equality between men and women.
11. SHETAUT NETER enjoins the justice for all.
12. SHETAUT NETER enjoins the sharing of resources.
13. SHETAUT NETER enjoins the protection and proper raising of children.
14. SHETAUT NETER enjoins the movement towards balance and peace.

Universality of Shetaut Neter

Shetaut Neter is the name or ancient African term that most likely you have heard translated as the "Egyptian Mysteries." You probably know that the Egyptian Mysteries is something that was practiced an Kamit (ancient Egypt). In general (orthodox) western culture, it is often related as something mysterious, something occult, something shrouded in history, in darkness. People are oftentimes told that they should shy away from it or that they should fear it. This is one of the great hoaxes that have been perpetrated on ancient Egyptian spirituality and African Culture. The importance of African philosophy is not only for African culture in Africa, but African Culture outside of Africa, the latter relating to all humanity in the larger sense. Most people in the world are following spiritual traditions and philosophies in ways that are leading them into ignorance, darkness, stress and strife. Those are not humanistic traditions, traditions that are based on truth and universal spirituality. We need to rectify this. Firstly, this philosophy is for all people. Our own Kamitan scriptures state this point. Shetaut Neter (The Egyptian Mysteries) is a universal teaching to improve life, and promote peace and prosperity for all. All people are part of the human family, spiritually and physically. Genetics has shown that all human beings, regardless of if one's ancestry is from Africa, Asia, Europe or the Americas in more recent times, all originated from Africa. Therefore, all human beings are Africans, sharing in the legacy and heritage of Africa. This fact was well recognized in ancient times. Therefore, Neterianism does not support any form of racism, sexism or notion of superiority of any individual, gender or group of humans being over another.

Being a Follower of Shetaut Neter

In order to become a follower of Shetaut Neter an aspirant must become a member of the Shemsu Congregation of converted devotees of Shetaut Neter.

What is the Philosophy of Shems?

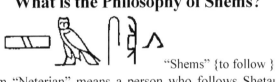

"Shems" {to follow }

The term "Neterian" means a person who follows Shetaut Neter, and the specific term for that person who is a "follower" is *Shems*. *Shemsu* are persons (plural) who follow Shetaut Neter. They are disciples or followers. This next slide shows the specific Medu Neter scripture that gives us this wisdom of the terms:

Shems means "follow." *Shemsu Shetaut Neter* are the followers of the Neterian Path. What does it mean to follow something? Why should some things be followed and others not? What should be followed in life and why? These are certainly some of the most important questions in life because if serious thought is put to them, they involve the crucial questions of life, who am I? Why am I here? What is my purpose? Which are or should be the most important concerns in life? This teaching of *Shems* offers some answers.

tu-a m shems n Neberdjer

Little Book of Neter

"I am a follower of Neberdjer

⟷ 𓄿𓏭𓏭 〰 𓊖⟷𓏏𓏭𓏭

er sesh n Kheperu

in accordance with the writings of Lord Kheperu"

In ancient times, Lord Khepri gave the spiritual teaching and then Lord Djehuti created *Medu Neter* (hieroglyphs) to write it down. Then Lord Asar created Shetaut Neter, the organized way to practice the teachings of the mysteries. And Heru, the son of Lord Asar became the supreme upholder of the teaching and all who follow Heru are on the glorious road that will lead them to discover the mysteries of life and the splendor of eternity. The answer to the important questions of life was given by the sages of ancient times as following the spiritual path. In ancient times that path was known as *Shetaut Neter*. These teachings were passed on through history to succeeding generations of sages, priestess and priestesses of Neterian Religion. So, why is it important for you to become a member of the Shetaut Neter tradition and what does it mean to be a follower of the Shetaut Neter spiritual teaching? If you are reading this it is because at one time or another you have come to the recognition of the important work being conducted by those who currently are following *Shetaut Neter* for the betterment of humanity but

also to promote your own 𓏤𓄿𓂧 *Nehast* {spiritual awakening and emancipation, resurrection}. In order to reach the state of consciousness known as *Nehast* there must first be

𓏤𓄿𓈖𓏏 *Nehas* {wakefulness, being awake}. Being awake implies wakefulness towards the teaching, that is, attentiveness, spending time, desire, etc. for spiritual pursuits. This means being mature enough to have grown beyond childish pursuits and interests, the worldly ideals of life. Needing to have a job to support oneself and one's family should not be an impediment to intensive practice. However, it will become an obstacle if that job or career is the main objective in life. The teaching should be the main objective and the job should be a means to finance the intensification of the practice of the teachings. Those who want to discover the true meaning of life should follow the teaching with practice that includes devotional practices, rituals, and the study of Maat

𓂝𓏲𓏭𓏭 teachings to develop purity or heart until a higher level of aspiration develops. The focus here is to develop ⌒ 𓋴𓏛𓊪 𓃭 *arit maat* {"offering righteous actions, living life righteously"}.

The opposite of *nehas* is 𓇋𓃀 𓁹 *Nem* {"sleep, slumber, slothfulness, immaturity"}. A person who is immature cannot adopt the teaching properly and will thus not be able to follow it rightly. What is needed is wakefulness towards higher perspectives in life and slothfulness towards what is degraded. This means an aspirant should learn to be awake as opposed to ordinary worldly people who are asleep towards the higher perspective and wakeful towards what is base, degraded and illusory in life. Once there is wakefulness, spiritual sensitivity, spiritual aspiration, respect for the sages and reverence towards the spiritual teaching and the Divine there should be 𓈖𓇋𓃀𓊪𓁹 *Snehas* {"Wakefulness, watchfulness, alertness, vigilance"}. There are many who follow spiritual teachings of all traditions who at times appear to have grown and at others seem to have fallen back to their old habits and degraded passions and desires *aba* 𓏭𓏛𓆱. In order to truly follow an ideal one must be steady on the path and watchful so that negative behaviors and patterns do not draw one back into earlier, lower states of consciousness.

The work of following a spiritual teaching requires the follower's financial support but also their psychic support as well as their physical support. When a person becomes a member they are taking an important step in sustaining the dissemination of the ⌒⌒ | | | *shetit*, "teachings" of 𓊃𓃀𓏤𓄿𓏤 *Shetaut Neter*- "Ancient Egyptian Religion" for themselves and for the world. As the membership grows and the pooling of resources increases, it will be possible to affect more lives and create more powerful programs to better facilitate the practice of the teachings. It is important to take the step of membership because this shows to oneself, the world and to others of like mind that there are others who believe, feel and aspire as they do and this develops *udja* 𓊝𓏏𓃀 spiritual strength and in a mysterious way allows every individual member to have a subtle means of support that urges them on to success on the spiritual path wherever they may be. So *shems* is the means to have 𓂝𓄿𓏏𓂋𓈖𓀭 *knumt-nefer* –"good association, divine association, joining others, together." This is a special association, unlike the worldly kinds of groups that have worldly goals and objective or religious goals and objectives. *Shems* is the coming together of followers of the Divine for the purpose of promoting righteousness and order in society and also spiritual awakening and enlightenment for those who are ready to tread the path to 𓂋𓐍𓅓𓄿𓃀 *rech-m-ab* –"self-knowledge, higher consciousness" and 𓈖𓈖𓂝𓏏𓋹 *an-menit* –"immortality."

Anyone can join the Shemsu if they sincerely desire to follow this path. Joining is an act of faith and it is done by expressing your desire to become a Neterian Follower. Those who formally join are called *Neterians* because they follow Shetaut Neter (Neterianism). Becoming part of the Shemsu means you will gain support from others who are trying to overcome immaturity but you also must put forth effort to act, think and speak with maturity and integrity. So those who want to put forth effort towards self-improvement and worthiness to progress in the teachings, should take the oath of Shetaut Neter. The oath is a pledge to apply yourself to the teaching of Shetaut Neter to your best capacity in order for its teaching to be revealed. Those who take the oath are considered as official followers of the Shetaut Neter Religion so it is a rite of conversion to Shetaut Neter. Becoming a follower is the first serious step on the path. The next is initiation. In order to take the oath it must be performed in the presence of a qualified priest or priestess of Shetaut Neter.

Also Shems means following or directing the attention and obeying the leader and the teachings of the tradition that is being followed. The following term 𓌞𓏤𓊪𓐍𓀀 means *Shemsu Heru* - Followers of Heru. This is the highest kind of title a Neterian aspirant can be given. Such a person is a true follower of the teaching, a true follower of God. Heru means "that which is most high."

The Supreme Being is One

> "God is the father of beings. God is the eternal One...
> and infinite and endures forever. God is hidden and no
> man knows God's form. No man has been able to seek
> out God's likeness. God is hidden to Gods and men...
> God's name remains hidden... It is a mystery to his
> children, men, women and Gods. God's names are
> innumerable, manifold and no one knows their number...
> though God can be seen in form and observation of God
> can be made at God's appearance, God cannot be
> understood... God cannot be seen with mortal eyes...
> God is invisible and inscrutable to Gods as well as men."
> -Portions from the Egyptian Book of Coming forth by
> Day and
> the papyrus of Nesi-Khensu

The statements above give the understanding that God is the
unfathomable mystery behind all phenomena, which cannot be discerned
"even by the gods." However, God is the unfathomable mystery as well
as the innermost essence of his children. This means that God is
transcendental, the unmanifest, but also what is manifest as well. In order
to perceive this reality it is necessary to transcend ordinary human vision.
When this transcendental Self is spoken about through different names
and metaphors, the idea often emerges that there are many faces to the
ultimate deity or Supreme Being. Nevertheless, as has been previously
discussed, it must be clear that all the Neterian spiritual traditions are in
reality referring to the same Supreme Being, the transcendental reality.

UA ⟨hieroglyphs⟩ or "One,"
UA NETER ⟨hieroglyphs⟩ or "One God,"
"Only One" ⟨hieroglyphs⟩,
"Only One Without a second"
⟨hieroglyphs⟩
"One One" ⟨hieroglyphs⟩

The following passages come from the Egyptian Book of Coming Forth
By Day (Chapter. clxxiii):

> "I praise thee, Lord of the Gods, God One, living in
> truth."

The following passage is taken from a hymn where princess Nesi-Khensu glorifies Amen-Ra:

> "August Soul which came into being in primeval time, the great god living in truth, the first Nine Gods who gave birth to the other two Nine Gods,[1] the being in whom every God existeth One One, ⸝⸝⸝⸝ the creator of the kings who appeared when the earth took form in the beginning, whose birth is hidden, whose forms are manifold, whose germination cannot be known."

The Companies of Gods and Goddesses

Before going on it is important to understand the Neterian concept of Pauti. Pauti means Company of Gods and Goddesses.

Study of the term "Pa"

By studying the phonetic and pictorial (Kamitan language is not only phonetic, but also illustrative) etymology (the origin and development of a linguistic form) and etiology (the study of causes or origins) of names and applying the initiatic science, it is possible to decipher the mysteries of Creation by discovering the teachings embedded in the language by the Sages of Ancient Egypt.

For example, the Kamitan word "Pa" is central to understanding the deeper essence of nature, divinity and the gods and goddesses of the Prt m Hru. In the study of the word "Pa," philosophy as well as pictorial and phonetic associations must be considered. Along with this, the variations in spellings act to expand the possible associations and thereby also the appropriate meaning in the given usage. Sometimes the very same words may be used, but its usage in different texts denotes a slight difference in the nuance of the meaning in accordance with the usage. This aspect of assigning the proper meaning of a word which is used even with the same spelling but in different contexts in different or even the same

---

[1] Ancient Egyptian mythology conceives of creation as an expression of God in which there are nine primordial cosmic principles or forces in the universe. These first nine may be seen as the cause from which all other qualities of nature *(the other two Nine Gods)* or creative forces in nature arise.

Kamitan scriptures, is an artistic development which comes to a translator with time. Thus, there is no right or wrong interpretation, but there is greater and greater approximation to the higher intended truth behind the teaching as research moves forward. Also, it should be remembered that research here implies not only studying books, but also meditation and introspection, as well as living in accordance with the philosophy.

The Ancient Egyptian words and symbols related to the Company of Gods and Goddesses (Pauti) indicate several important mystical teachings. The root of the Ancient Egyptian word Pauti is Pa (Figure A-Above). Pa means "to exist." Thus, Creation is endowed with the quality of existence as opposed to non-existence. Pau (Figure B) is the next progression in the word. It means the Primeval Divinity, the source of Creation. Paut (Figure C and D) is the next evolution of the word, Pau, meaning primeval time and the very substance out of which everything is created is the one and the same. Pauti is the next expression of **Pa** and it has two major meanings. It refers to the Primeval Divinity or Divine Self (God) (Figure E). Pautiu refers to Pauti but in plural, as well as being a gender specific term implying, the Divinity as the source of the multiplicity in creation. In the Ancient Egyptian language, like Spanish for example, all objects are assigned gender. Also, Pauti refers to the deities who comprise the Company of Gods and Goddesses (Figure G and H). Paut (men) or Pautet (women) also refers to living beings, especially human beings (Figure I).

Pa ➔ Pau ➔ Paut ➔ Pauti ➔ Pautiu ➔ Paut and Pautet

Therefore, the most important teaching relating to the nature of Creation is being given here. The gods and goddesses of the creation are not separate principles or entities. They are in reality one and the same as the Primeval Divinity. They are expressions of that Divine Self. However, they are not transformations of or evolutions from the Divine Self, but the very same Divine Self expressing as Creation. So even though God is referred to as a primordial deity who did something a long time ago or set into motion various things, in reality God and Creation are one and the same. Ra is the "God of the primeval time" as well as the gods and goddesses of Creation which sustain it all the time. With this understanding, it is clear to see that God is not distant and aloof, observing Creation from afar. The Divine Self is the very basis of Creation and is in every part of it at all times. This is why the terms *Pa-Neter* and *Neteru* are also used to describe the Divine. Pa-Neter means "The Supreme Being" and Neteru means "the gods and goddesses."

Also, the word "Neteru" refers to creation itself. So Neter-u emanates from Neter. Creation is nothing but God who has assumed various forms or Neteru: trees, cake, bread, human beings, metal, air, fire, water, animals, planets, space, electricity, etc. This is a profound teaching which should be reflected upon constantly so that the mind may become enlightened to its deeper meaning and thereby discover the Divinity in nature. The Divine Self is not only in Creation but is the very essence of every human being as well. Therefore, the substratum of every human being is in reality God as well. The task of spiritual practice and Yoga is to discover this essential nature within your own heart. This can occur if one reflects upon this teaching and realizes its meaning by discovering its reality in the deepest recesses of one's own experience. When this occurs, the person who has attained this level of self-discovery is referred to as having become enlightened. They have discovered their true, divine nature. They have discovered their oneness with the Divine Self.

The ultimate truth is that when we speak of objects, we are in reality speaking about principles, deeper basis of which is the Divine Self. When words are spoken, they immediately take on the first level of reality as they engender an image in the mind of the listener. When a listener acts upon what has been heard, the speech takes on a reality in the physical plane. Therefore, the speech is a reflection of an idea, a concept, and the physical reality is a reflection of speech. The cause underlying the concept is the real name of a thing, its higher reality, and this essence has no name or form in its potentiality, but only in its relative manifestation. This relative manifestation is the world of time and space and all living and non-living objects in it. Therefore, we have three levels of reality, the thought, the word and the actual object existing in the physical world. However, these are only relative realities since they are all ephemeral in nature and not abiding. The creative essence (God-transcendental consciousness) which gave power to the thought, the concept, is the source and substratum which lends temporary reality to the projection (thought, the word and the actual object).

Neter and the Neteru

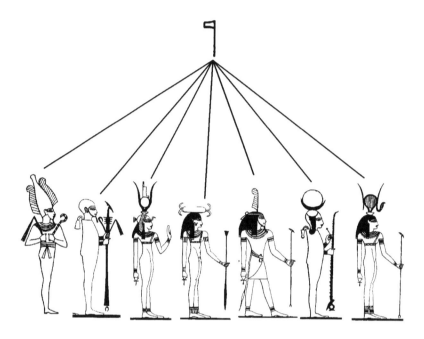

The concept of Neter and Neteru binds and ties all of the varied forms of Kamitan spirituality into one vision of the gods and goddesses all emerging from the same Supreme Being. Therefore, ultimately. Kamitan spirituality is not polytheistic, nor is it monotheistic, for it holds that the Supreme Being is more than a God but an all-encompassing Absolute Divinity.

"Neteru"

The term "Neteru" means "gods and goddesses." This means that from the ultimate and transcendental Supreme Being, "Neter," come the Neteru. There are countless Neteru. So from the one come the many. These Neteru are cosmic forces that pervade the universe. They are the means by which Neter sustains Creation and manifests through it. So Neterianism is a monotheistic polytheism. The one Supreme Being expresses as many gods and goddesses and at the end of time, after their work of sustaining Creation is finished, these gods and goddesses are again absorbed back into the Supreme Being.

All of the spiritual systems of Ancient Egypt (Kamit) have one essential aspect that is common to all; They all hold that there is a Supreme Being (Neter) who manifests in a multiplicity of ways through nature, the Neteru.

Like sunrays, the Neteru emanate from the Divine and they are its manifestations. So by studying the Neteru we learn about and are led to discover their source, the Neter. And with this discovery we are enlightened.

The Neteru may be depicted anthropomorphically or zoomorphically in accordance with the teaching about Neter that is being conveyed through them

Six Main Traditions of Shetaut Neter

Six Main Traditions of *Shetaut Neter*

Shetaut Anu – Teachings of the Ra Tradition
Shetaut Menefer –Teachings of the Ptah Tradition
Shetaut Waset – Teachings of the Amun Tradition
Shetaut Netrit– Teachings of the Goddess Tradition
Shetaut Asar – Teachings of the Asarian Tradition
Shetaut Aton – Teachings of the Aton Tradition

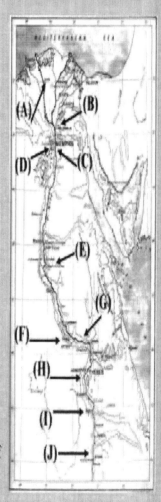

The cities wherein the major theologies developed were:

A. Sais (temple of Net),
B. Anu (Heliopolis- temple of Ra),
C. Men-nefer or Hetkaptah (Memphis, temple of Ptah),
D. Sakkara (Pyramid Texts),
E. Akhet-Aton (City of Akhenaton, temple of Aton),
F. Abdu (temple of Asar),
G. Denderah (temple of Hetheru),
H. Waset (Thebes, temple of Amun),
I. Edfu (temple of Heru),
J. Philae (temple of Aset). The cities wherein the theology of the Trinity of Asar-Aset-Heru was developed were Anu, Abydos, Philae, Edfu, Denderah and Edfu.

There are six main traditions of Shetaut Neter. Shetaut Neter is the all-encompassing national name to refer to the religious program of life of Ancient Kamit. It is a general term. Within that general reference meaning "Ancient Egyptian Religion" there are six main traditions of spirituality. They are all related. So there is no conflict between them. In fact all of them emerge from a single one, which is Anunian Theology, Shetaut Anu.

All the other ones emanate from this one. You should not think of them as sects in the context of Christian sects, like Presbyterians versus Pentecostals, or the Pentecostals versus the Catholics or something like that. This would be more like branches within one spiritual tradition.

Paut Neteru
The Company of Gods and Goddesses of Ancient Egypt

These traditions relate to different forms of spiritual practice; that is why they were devised. Some are more psychologically oriented, some more ritualistic, and some deal more with the wisdom aspect, and so on and so forth, to accommodate the different inclinations of different personality types. And they were spread out throughout the different main cities of Ancient Kamit, to serve the need of the different parts of the population.

Within those six traditions there are three main theologies. These are based on the Great Trinity of Amun, Ra, and Ptah, which is also the basis of the chant that we use: *Om, Amun-Ra-Ptah.*

The branches of Neterian theologies:

In the center of the slide (above) you can see the Ra tradition, the Anunian Theology or tradition (a). The Ptah Theology or tradition is identified by (b), and the Amun Theology or tradition by (c). This slide illustrates that the Anunian Theology gave rise to the Divinities in both of the branches (Wasetian {Theban} and Menefer {Memphite}). Thus, the Divinities from the Ptah Theology arise from the Anunian Theology and the Divinities from the Amun Theology also emerge from the Anunian Theology. The Asarian Tradition is another branch which also emerges from Anunian Theology. The Asarian Tradition is based on the divinities Asar, Aset, and Heru, (Osiris, Isis, and Horus). It is from this tradition that the Christian myth develops.   This slide illustrates that though there are many gods and goddesses in the Neterian Theology, called Neteru, they all emanate from the single Supreme Being. The group of gods and goddesses are called Paut (group of gods and goddesses) or Pautti (groups of gods and goddesses).   All the gods and goddesses emanate from the single One.

The Anunian Tradition

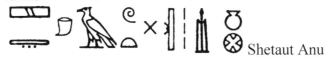 Shetaut Anu

The Mystery Teachings of the Anunian Tradition are related to the Divinity Ra and his company of Gods and Goddesses.[2] This Temple and its related Temples espouse the teachings of Creation, human origins and the path to spiritual enlightenment by means of the Supreme Being in the form of the god Ra. It tells of how Ra emerged from a primeval ocean and how human beings were created from his tears. The gods and goddesses, who are his children, go to form the elements of nature and the cosmic forces that maintain nature.

Top: Ra. From top and left to right, The Gods and Goddesses of Anunian Theology:
      Ra, Shu, Tefnut, Geb, Nut, Aset, Asar, Set, Nebthet and Heru-Ur

---

[2] See the Book Anunian Theology by Muata Ashby

The Theban Tradition

 **Shetaut Amun**

The Mystery Teachings of the Wasetian Tradition are related to the Neterus known as Amun, Mut Khonsu. This temple and its related temples espoused the teachings of Creation, human origins and the path to spiritual enlightenment by means of the Supreme Being in the form of the god Amun or Amun-Ra. It tells of how Amun and his family, the Trinity of Amun, Mut and Khonsu, manage the Universe along with his Company of Gods and Goddesses. This Temple became very important in the early part of the New Kingdom Era.

Below: The Trinity of Amun and the Company of Gods and Goddesses of Amun

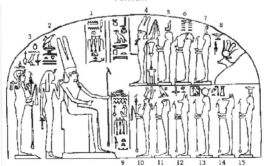

See the Book *Egyptian Yoga Vol. 2* for more on Amun, Mut and Khonsu by Muata Ashby

43

The Goddess Tradition

Shetaut Netrit

"Arat"

The hieroglyphic sign Arat means "Goddess." General, throughout ancient Kamit, the Mystery Teachings of the Goddess Tradition are related to the Divinity in the form of the Goddess. The Goddess was an integral part of all the Neterian traditions but special temples also developed around the worship of certain particular Goddesses who were also regarded as Supreme Beings in their own right. Thus as in other African religions, the goddess as well as the female gender were respected and elevated as the male divinities. The Goddess was also the author of Creation, giving birth to it as a great Cow. The following are the most important forms of the goddess.[3]

Aset, Net, Sekhmit, Mut, Hetheru

Mehurt ("The Mighty Full One")

---

[3] See the Books, *The Goddess Path, Mysteries of Aset, Glorious Light Meditation, Memphite Theology* and *Resurrecting Asar* by Muata Ashby

The Asarian Tradition

 **Shetaut Asar**

This temple and its related temples espoused the teachings of Creation, human origins and the path to spiritual enlightenment by means of the Supreme Being in the form of the god Asar. It tells of how Asar and his family, the Trinity of Asar, Aset and Heru, manage the Universe and lead human beings to spiritual enlightenment and the resurrection of the soul. This Temple and its teaching were very important from the Pre-Dynastic era down to the Christian period. The Mystery Teachings of the Asarian Tradition are related to the Neterus known as: Asar, Aset, Heru (Asar, Aset and Heru)

The tradition of Asar, Aset and Heru was practiced generally throughout the land of ancient Kamit. The centers of this tradition were the city of Abdu containing the Great Temple of Asar, the city of Pilak containing the Great Temple of Aset[4] and Edfu containing the Ggreat Temple of Heru.

---

[4] See the Book Resurrecting Asar by Muata Ashby

The Aton Tradition

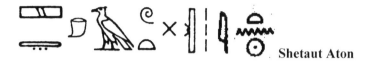

Shetaut Aton

This temple and its related temples espoused the teachings of Creation, human origins and the path to spiritual enlightenment by means of the Supreme Being in the form of the god Aton. It tells of how Aton with its dynamic life force created and sustains Creation. By recognizing Aton as the very substratum of all existence, human beings engage in devotional exercises and rituals and the study of the Hymns containing the wisdom teachings of Aton explaining that Aton manages the Universe and leads human beings to spiritual enlightenment and eternal life for the soul. This Temple and its teaching were very important in the middle New Kingdom Period. The Mystery Teachings of the Aton Tradition are related to the Neter Aton and its main exponent was the Sage King Akhnaton, who is depicted below with his family adoring the sundisk, symbol of the Aton.

Akhnaton, Nefertiti and Daughters

For more on Atonism and the Aton Theology see the Essence of Atonism Lecture Series by Sebai Muata Ashby ©2001

The Memphite Tradition

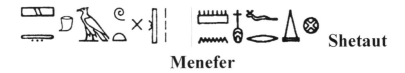 **Shetaut**

Menefer

The Mystery Teachings of the Menefer (Memphite) Tradition are related to the Neterus known as Ptah, Sekhmit, Nefertem. The myths and philosophy of these divinities constitutes Memphite Theology.[5] This temple and its related temples espoused the teachings of Creation, human origins and the path to spiritual enlightenment by means of the Supreme Being in the form of the god Ptah and his family, who compose the Memphite Trinity. It tells of how Ptah emerged from a primeval ocean and how he created the universe by his will and the power of thought (mind). The gods and goddesses who are his thoughts, go to form the elements of nature and the cosmic forces that maintain nature. His spouse, Sekhmit has a powerful temple system of her own that is related to the Memphite teaching. The same is true for his son Nefertem.

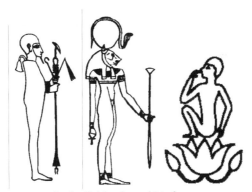

Ptah, Sekhmit and Nefertem

---

[5] See the Book Memphite Theology by Muata Ashby

47

The Forces of Entropy in Shetaut Neter Religious Traditions

In Neterian religion, there is no concept of "evil" as is conceptualized in Western Culture. Rather, it is understood that the forces of entropy are constantly working in nature to bring that which has been constructed by human hands to their original natural state. The serpent Apep (Apophis), who daily tries to stop Ra's boat of creation, is the symbol of entropy. This concept of entropy has been referred to as "chaos" by Western Egyptologists.

Apep

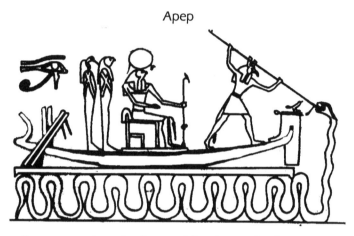

Above: Set protecting the boat of Ra from the forces of entropy (symbolized by the serpent Apep).

As expressed previously, in Neterian religion there is also no concept of a "devil" or "demon" as is conceived in the Judeo-Christian or Islamic traditions. Rather, it is understood that manifestations of detrimental situations and adversities arise as a result of unrighteous actions. These unrighteous actions are due to the "Setian" qualities in a human being. Set is the Neteru of egoism and the negative qualities which arise from egoism. Egoism is the idea of individuality based on identification with the body and mind only as being who one is. One has no deeper awareness of their deeper spiritual essence, and thus no understanding of their connectedness to all other objects (includes persons) in creation and the Divine Self. When the ego is under the control of the higher nature, it fights the forces of entropy (as above). However, when beset with ignorance, it leads to the degraded states of human existence. The vices (egoism, selfishness, extraverted ness, wonton sexuality (lust), jealousy, envy, greed, gluttony) are a result.

Set

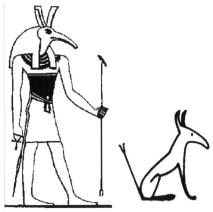

Set and the Set animal

Nehast means to "wake up," to Awaken to the higher existence. In the Prt m Hru Text it is said:

Nuk pa Neter aah Neter Zjah asha ren

"I am that same God, the Supreme One, who has myriad of mysterious names."

The goal of all the Neterian disciplines is to discover the meaning of "Who am I?," to unravel the mysteries of life and to fathom the depths of eternity and infinity. This is the task of all human beings and it is to be accomplished in this very lifetime.

This can be done by learning the ways of the Neteru, emulating them and finally becoming like them, Akhus, (enlightened beings), walking the earth as giants and accomplishing great deeds such as the creation of the universe!

Udjat
The Eye of Heru is a quintessential symbol of awakening to Divine Consciousness, representing the concept of Nehast.

---

[6] (Prt M Hru 9:4)

SCRIPTURES OF SHETAUT NETER

There are three kinds of scriptures in Kamitan culture. We have Mythic scriptures, Mystical scriptures, and Wisdom Text scriptures. In addition to these, there is also the genre of the Harper's songs. Though belonging in the category of music, they are also to be considered as part of the wisdom literature. The main mythic texts of Shetaut Neter are the *PertmHeru (Egyptian Book of Enlightenment), Hessu Amun (Hymns of Amun), Sebait menefer (Memphite Theology).* All the books that I have written are based on these scriptures. Some of you have been amazed by the extensive writings that I have brought forth in reference to the Neterian teachings. Well, I have not invented them; they are not fabricated. The teachings are based on our own scriptures, our own traditions, and our own ancestry. So I believe we do not have to look beyond the original scriptures for records of the teachings. We don't have to invent them, and we don't have to speculate about them. We can confirm this because you can see the tradition being practiced by other African cultures. What I mean is that they are practicing the rituals and customs, but not necessarily understanding the meaning. If they were to study the true depth of the Neterian Spirituality, they would realize the deeper meaning of the rituals and traditions they have kept for so long. You see parts of Neterianism being practiced in the Western religions, and also in Asia, in Hinduism and Buddhism, which have their origins in Neterian theology. For more on this see the book *African Origins.*

Neterian Initiations

There are three major forms of Neterian Initiation.

Initiation is the ancient tradition of ritual and process of initiating your steps on the chosen spiritual path. It is a personal choice to enter into a spiritual tradition and relationship with a specific teaching and preceptor who will lead you to discover the nature of Self. It is a means to facilitate your ability to assimilate the teaching and it is a more powerful way to practice spirituality as opposed to studying on your own. Initiation strengthens your bonds to the teaching and the teacher and psycho-mythologically redirects your personality to become a proper vessel for the teaching.

SHEMSU INITIATION

Level 1- The first is the Shemsu Initiation is open to anyone who wants to adopt Neterianism. This is the neophyte   level. Shemsu means follower, one who has adopted the path of Shetaut Neter and their religion, their personal spiritual path. There are varied levels of initiation into the temple. Birth is an initiation into life, which is presided over by parents. They provide a person their cultural name and general conditions for life. What a human being does with those conditions is up to them, through their actions. This is what makes human beings have the capacity to stand above nature. One of the ways of affirming your decision to move towards your chosen path is changing your cultural or ethnic name. At this level many neophytes choose a cultural name that reflects their Kamitan aspirations. Neophytes must learn the Great Truths of Shetaut Neter and the Neterian Creed.

The Oath of the Shemsu of Shetaut Neter?

In order to become a follower, an aspirant of Shetaut Neter a person must:

Resolve to have faith in the Neterian path as laid out by Lord Heru.
Resolve to listen to the teaching of Shemsu and study it's meaning.
Resolve to practice the threefold worship daily.
Resolve to practice the teachings of Maat in your day-to-day life to your best ability.

Take the oath of Shems- pledge your faith to the Neterian Path and the teachings of Lord Heru.
After making the offering of incense, water libation, food, over an image or icon of Lord Heru, repeat the oath 7 times (From the PertmHeru text, Chap 1 verse 7).

nua   amtu –   k   Heru
I am one of those who support and believe in Heru. (Repeat Seven Times)

TEMPLE INITIATION
Level 2-The second is the Temple Initiation– The Temple Initiation or Asar Initiation is for those who want to be temple level practitioners of the path of Shetaut Neter, engaging in intensive *Shedy* studies of the mysteries. At this level the aspirant formally receives the Temple Initiate name.

HEMU INITIATION

Level 3-The Hemu Initiation or priesthood initiation is the level for those who want to seriously dedicate their lives to the path of Shetaut Neter as priests and priestesses and to teach it to others. The first level of priesthood is UNUT and is open to mature men and women.

GREAT TRUTHS OF SHETAUT NETER

An aspirant should begin to gain an understanding of the integral aspects of Shetaut Neter religion even as the myths and disciplines are studied and as the teachings are practiced. In this manner, the serious aspirant may begin to absorb the wisdom of the teachings by receiving varied elements in small doses so as to comprehend them well as develop a keen intellect and a purified personality. Some of the most important and essential teachings of Shetaut Neter are contained in the Four Great Truth statements. Read these over and over again and as you read the books the teaching of the Four Truths will become clearer. For a more detailed explanation of the 4 Great Truths of Shetaut Neter see the book Egyptian Mysteries Vol. 1.

I

"The Neter, the Supreme Being, is One and alone and as Neberdjer, manifesting everywhere and in all things in the form of Gods and Goddesses."

II

"Lack of righteousness brings fetters to the personality and these fetters cause ignorance of the Divine."

III

"Devotion to the Divine leads to freedom from the fetters of Set."

IIII

"The practice of the Shedy disciplines leads to knowing oneself and the Divine. This is called being True of Speech"

NETERIANISM AND WESTERN RELIGION

If anyone refers to Ancient Egyptian or African Religion as polytheistic, that is an incorrect assessment. Such persons did not study ancient African Religion; it may be that they are ignorant or did not care to study, or to understand. If they understood this, then they would have to give Ancient Egyptian (African) Religion its due respect. With respect to those in other religions who propagate this erroneous idea (of polytheism), their acknowledgement of this truth would require that they admit that they are not the only ones with a so called elevated notions or advanced conception of religion. It would mean that someone else is as civilized as they are, and maybe even more advanced. This realization is hard for degraded, egoistic personalities to accept. So their reaction is often to denigrate, disparage, marginalize and ridicule anything contrary to their own beliefs, ideas and concepts, so that they may continue to feel good about themselves. They need that form of egoistic notion of superiority in order to compensate for the low self-esteem and low culture of human development that is based on material accomplishments. So it is fitting that western religions should be so based in the historicity of the myths of the western religions. That is a reflection of the materialistic nature of those societies. In other words, those types of religions are materialistic and consequently idolatrous. Yes, contrary to their own beliefs, western religions practice idolatry because they tend to concretize the Divine into one image, one proprietary culture, one sacred scripture, etc. This act of confining God into a materialistic concept is indeed idolatry. Further, these religions/cultures support the worship of objects not as expressions of the Divine as in African and Eastern religions, but as worthy objects that can bring happiness, even to the point of killing to preserve or acquire them. They are not viewed as The God, but rather, as a lesser manifestation that can be used to gain entry into the transcendental plane of consciousness. In materialistic type of societies, money, power, image, etc. become the gods and goddesses that people worship, and therefore, they are leading themselves down the road of pain and frustration. Those objects can never bring abiding happiness as they are evanescent, limited objects. Worshipping such objects is actually a very degraded form of human culture. The Neterian-African notion of religion is actually superior because it actually divinizes the entire creation. All of these gods and goddesses of Anunian Theology represent the elements of Creation. Earth is Geb. The sky, the heavens is Nut. Water is Tefnut, and air and space is Shu. With this kind of a notion, you cannot take a step outside of creation, outside of the Divinity. I am walking on Geb, I am breathing in Shu, I look up at the sky I see Nut. Where is Divinity not present? The entire Creation is the Temple then.

What is not readily visible is the Shetaut, "The hidden Divine Self." What we see here is called Bes. Bes means "outer image." We cannot see the hidden, because the hidden Divinity is transcendental, and we cannot see that with mortal eyes. Yet it sustains that which is visible in this time and space reality.

In western culture you do not have lesser beings or gods and goddesses per se. You are supposed to revere God or Jesus directly. But you cannot be as good as Jesus; there is really no one who can be as perfect as Christians would like. Consequently, everything is a guilt trip. As a Christian, seemingly everything you do is wrong, everything you do is upsetting... everything you do is a problem from the beginning – thus the concept of being born in sin. So consequently, Christians have to be seeking forgiveness all the time. In this way one cannot have a full communion with the Divine and discover true purity of heart that brings virtue. There is always that separation, that beholding nature, that inferiority complex that never seems to go away. But western religions do have intermediaries, saints and angels, which are essentially the same as gods and goddesses, even though they are not referred to in the same way or treated the same way. It is therefore hypocritical for proponents of western religions to look down on non-western religions when they doing the same thing.

So in the Kamitan system everything is divine. You understand everything as spiritual energy, a spiritual cosmic force that you are living in and working through, and trying to master. In mastering these forces, then you transcend their influences. Therefore you are not innately controlled by nature; you are potentially a master of nature. The Neterian systems of divinities give us easier entry into spirituality, because we could start with a turtle god of the river or Hapi, the Nile, and then that leads us to his relatives, and ultimately to the Supreme Being, Her/Himself. Furthermore, the divinities represent principles in nature and in our personalities that we need to control. Their propitiation removes egoism and ignorance, making it easier for the aspirant to grasp, and therefore understand and control the personality, so as to purify and realize the higher essence within. So the worship and study of those divinities is actually a study of our own constitution, our own psychological makeup (psyche) and our own spiritual architecture and the architecture of the universe. And this is why Neterian religion has many gods and goddesses. It is a scientific approach to allow a person to propitiate the Divine, leading them in an elevating process, to discover the Supreme Being. So this is not degraded religion at all; actually it is advanced religion.

What the Kamitan Mysteries Are Not

It is important to understand that the Egyptian Mysteries are not teachings originated by or controlled by organizations which in modern times refer to themselves as fraternal orders, lodges, masons, freemasons, illuminati, Odd Fellows, Shriners, new world orders, Satanists, occultists, or psychics.

Aspirants should be careful when examining the use of Kamitan symbols by modern organizations. For example, the use of the pyramid on the reverse of the seal of the United States would seem to mean that the founding fathers had the idea of invoking the principles of the Kamitan tradition in the founding of the new country. It was explained by the occultist and reputed expert in Masonic lore, Manly Hall, that many of the U.S. founding fathers were masons and that they received assistance from masons in Europe to establish the United States for "a peculiar and particular purpose known only to the initiated few." Hall said that the seal was the signature of the masons and that the unfinished pyramid symbolizes the task that the government has to accomplish. The eagle is a representation of the phoenix, which is the ancient Greek reinterpretation of the Kamitan Benu bird. Another Kamitan symbol used to represent the United States is the Washington Monument, which is a copy of the Ancient Egyptian Obelisk. The Lincoln memorial and Mount Rushmore, two of the most important icons of the United States were admittedly inspired by the Temple of Rameses II at Abu Simbel.

So the question may be asked, if they intended to use Kamitan representation which essentially means that they are wishing to adopt their meaning and symbolism, why then did the "founding fathers" of the government of the United States of America allow a government to be set up that is in almost complete contradiction with Kamitan principles?

Where to Go From Here?

Now you have been introduced to the spiritual path of Shetaut Neter. What is your next step? If you want to continue on this journey get the following books and read them in the following order.

Egyptian Mysteries: VOL. 1, Shetaut Neter ISBN: 1-884564-41-0 $19.99
Inmate Price $14.00
What are the Mysteries? For thousands of years the spiritual tradition of Ancient Egypt, S*hetaut Neter*, "The Egyptian Mysteries," "The Secret Teachings," have fascinated, tantalized and amazed the world. At one time exalted and recognized as the highest culture of the world, by Africans, Europeans, Asiatics, Hindus, Buddhists and other cultures of the ancient world, in time it was shunned by the emerging orthodox world religions. Its temples desecrated, its philosophy maligned, its tradition spurned, its philosophy dormant in the mystical *Medu Neter*, the mysterious hieroglyphic texts which hold the secret symbolic meaning that has scarcely been discerned up to now. What are the secrets of *Nehast* {spiritual awakening and emancipation, resurrection}. More than just a literal translation, this volume is for awakening to the secret code *Shetitu* of the teaching which was not deciphered by Egyptologists, nor could be understood by ordinary spiritualists. This book is a reinstatement of the original science made available for our times, to the reincarnated followers of Ancient Egyptian culture and the prospect of spiritual freedom to break the bonds of *Khemn*, "ignorance," and slavery to evil forces: *Såaa* .

INITIATION INTO EGYPTIAN YOGA
The Secrets of Sheti

New Expanded Edition with Study Group Guide
Sheti: Spiritual discipline or program, to go deeply into the mysteries, to study the mystery teachings and literature profoundly, to penetrate the mysteries.
GYou will learn about the mysteries of initiation into the teachings and practice of Yoga and how to become an Initiate of the mystical sciences. This insightful manual is the first in a series which introduces you to the goals of daily spiritual and yoga practices: Meditation, Diet, Words of Power and the ancient wisdom teachings.
ISBN 1-884564-04-6 $24.95

THE KEMETIC DIET
Food for the Body, Mind and Soul Size: 8 1/2" X 11"
$28.95 U.S. Inmate Price $20.00
ISBN: 1-884564-49-6
CLEANSING, HEALING, ENLIGHTENMENT OF BODY, MIND AND

SOUL!
Now available – Kemetic Diet Counseling – call for details or see web site www.Egyptianyoga.com
Health issues have always been important to human beings since the beginning of time. The earliest records of history show that knowledge of proper diet, preventative health practices, and the art of healing were held in high esteem since the time of Ancient Egypt (5,000 B.C.E. or before). Natural health concepts and healing techniques which were practiced in Ancient Egypt are now referred to as "alternative medicine" disciplines. They include those healing modalities which do not adhere to the philosophy of allopathic medicine, with its emphasis on masking the symptoms of disease with drugs rather than eliminating the root cause of disease. Allopathic treatment methods have shown their limitations over the years because they do not heal the entire person. This new volume presents the concepts and teachings based on the Kemetic (Ancient Egyptian) philosophy of total health of the entire person, that is, health not just of the body, but also health of the mind and soul as well, which gets to the root cause of the dis-ease and eradicates it. For this kind of health one must have a keen understanding of the body-mind-soul connection and, what it means to be truly healthy. Health is a lifestyle, not a medicine. It is a spiritual lifestyle that leads to health of body, mind and soul and ultimately to discovery of the Higher Self.

THE AFRICAN ORIGINS OF CIVILIZATION, RELIGION, MYSTICISM AND YOGA PHILOSOPHY
ISBN: 1-884564-50-X

HARD COVER ALL VOLUMES IN ONE
8½" X 11"   Over 683 Pages $45.00 <u>Inmate Price $36.00</u>

Where did Egyptian Yoga come from and who are its practitioners?
When did it develop and what is its lineage?
What is the Tradition of Egyptian Yoga?
Over the past several years I have been asked to put together in one volume the most important evidences showing the correlations and common teachings between Kemetic (Ancient Egyptian) culture and religion and that of India. The questions of the history of Ancient Egypt, and the latest archeological evidences showing civilization and culture in Ancient Egypt and its spread to other countries, has intrigued many scholars as well as mystics over the years.

FOR MORE BOOKS AND INFORMATION GO TO:

www.Egyptianyoga.com

Little Book of Neter

Order Form

Telephone orders: Call Toll Free: 1(305) 378-6253. Have your AMEX, Optima, Visa or MasterCard ready.

Fax orders: 1-(305) 378-6253   E-MAIL ADDRESS: Semayoga@aol.com

Postal Orders: Sema Institute of Yoga, P.O. Box 570459, Miami, Fl. 33257. USA.

Please send the following books and / or tapes.

ITEM

_____Cost $_____

_____Cost $_____

_____Cost $_____

_____Cost $_____

_____Cost $_____

Total $_____

Name:_____

Physical Address:_____

City:_____ State:_____ Zip:_____

Sales tax: Please add 6.5% for books shipped to Florida addresses
_____Shipping: $6.50 for first book and .50¢ for each additional
_____Shipping: Outside US $5.00 for first book and $3.00 for each additional

_____Payment:_____
_____Check -Include Driver License #:

_____

_____Credit card: _____ Visa, _____ MasterCard, _____ Optima,
_____ AMEX.

Card number:_____
Name on card:_____ Exp. date:_____/_____

Copyright 1995-2005 Dr. R. Muata Abhaya Ashby
Sema Institute of Yoga
P.O.Box 570459, Miami, Florida, 33257
(305) 378-6253 Fax: (305) 378-6253

Made in the USA
Middletown, DE
20 January 2017